Grandpa Doesn't Know It's Me

by Donna Guthrie

illustrated by Katy Keck Arnsteen

In cooperation with Alzheimer's Disease and Related Disorders Association, Inc.

A.D.™ Alzheimer's Disease
and Related Disorders Association, Inc.

HUMAN SCIENCES PRESS, INC.
72 FIFTH AVENUE
NEW YORK, N.Y. 10011

Dedicated to Flo Carris
—D.G.

Printed in the United States of America
987654321

Library of Congress Cataloging in Publication Data

Guthrie, Donna.
Grandpa doesn't know it's me.
Summary: Elizabeth observes her grandfather become a victim of
Alzheimer's disease and describes its symptoms and effects.
1. Alzheimer's disease—Juvenile literature.
2. Grandfathers—Care and hygiene—Juvenile literature.
3. Aged—Diseases—Juvenile literature.
[1. Alzheimer's disease. 2. Grandfathers. 3. Aged—Diseases]
I. Title.
RC523.G87   1986   618.97′683   85-30550
ISBN 0-89885-302-8
ISBN 0-89885-308-7 (pbk.)

A Note to Parents

This book is geared to concerns of the young child having a relative with Alzheimer's disease. It is designed to begin to answer some of the questions that arise: What is wrong? Is this an illness that happens to lots of grownups? Did I do anything to cause it? Will *you* get it? Will I get it? Why did it happen to *us*? What do I tell my friends? Most of all, it is a first step in communication. It opens up dialogue for the child with his or her family so that more questions can be brought out as the need is felt over the passage of time, making it easier for the child to come to terms with the situation. In this experience, for which the child is not responsible, he or she still can play an active role. "There is no cure" needn't mean there's nothing *to do*.

It is heart-breaking to watch a loved one deteriorate slowly and change his or her personality and roles. For instance, a powerful decisive figure in the business world may become an insecure, dependent, almost childlike figure. It is hard to accept that a still healthy-looking individual can no longer perform even the most routine daily personal activities such as feeding, bathing, grooming, and toileting. If this is baffling for an adult, imagine how confusing it may be for a young child— not only confusing, but perhaps embarrassing and frightening as well.

Alzheimer's disease is the single most common cause of progressive intellectual decline—that is, dementing illness in adults.* A neurological illness, Alzheimer's disease, named for the German doctor who identified it in 1907, first affects memory and other intellectual functions, robbing its victims of their uniquely human capacities, and eventually of life itself. It is a mysterious disease: it is insidious; its symptoms are vague; it affects the mind long before it debilitates the body. Its cause is unknown and there is, at present, no cure. There are 2.5 million affected persons, but many more victims— families, friends, neighbors of patients—even society itself is robbed of productive individuals and also must provide resources for care.

Miriam K. Aronson, Ed.D.
*Educational Consultant, Alzheimer's Disease
and Related Disorders Association*

*Associate Professor of Neurology and Psychiatry
Albert Einstein College of Medicine
Bronx, New York 10461*

*To aid families encountering this problem, a national organization, Alzheimer's Disease and Related Disorders Association, established in 1980, is dedicated to providing family support, improving education and public awareness, promoting research toward finding a cure, and encouraging the development of needed assistance for victims and their families. This organization has a nationwide network of Chapters and family support groups. For more information about the disease and about Chapter and family support groups in your own area, write Alzheimer's Disease and Related Disorders Association at 70 East Lake Street, Chicago, Illinois 60601, or call its toll-free number: 1-800-621-0379, or in Illinois, 1-800-572-6037.

Down the street is a little gray house where my
Grandpa used to live. A swing still hangs in the
tallest tree. Grandpa made it for me.

He would push me high into the air and I could
see over the rosebushes into his garden.

Grandpa taught me lots of things. When I was little, he taught me how to ride my big wheel. I would zoom down the sidewalk and Grandpa would run behind me saying, "Slow down, Lizzie, slow down!"

When I got my two-wheeler Grandpa and I rode around the neighborhood together.

Grandpa and I did lots of things together. We'd trim the rosebushes, feed the birds, and sit on his front porch and watch the squirrels. He told me stories about the funny things my Daddy did when he was a little boy.

I loved being with Grandpa.

In first grade, Dad took the training wheels off my bicycle. I rode over to Grandpa's house to show him.

"Come ride with me, Grandpa!" I called.

"Not today," he said, sadly. "I just don't feel like riding." He didn't want to ride bikes with me anymore. He just wanted to sit and watch.

Grandpa began forgetting things. He would talk about times long ago as if they happened yesterday.

"I remember when I bought my first car. It was a shiny red convertible with lots of chrome," he'd say.

But he couldn't remember things that happened now. Sometimes he'd forget people's names, or where he put things, or what he was planning to do next.

"Now, what am I doing in here?" he'd ask. "What was I going to do?"

One day we went to the grocery store and Grandpa forgot what he wanted to buy.

"All that way to the store and I didn't even need anything," he said. We laughed and joked all the way home.

It didn't matter that Grandpa forgot things. They were usually things that didn't matter much.

But one day after school, when I went to Grandpa's house, I found a pot burning on the kitchen stove. Grandpa had opened a can of soup for lunch, turned on the stove, and walked off. The soup boiled away and smoked up the kitchen.

That night at dinner, I told Mom and Dad.

"I don't like the idea of Grandpa living by himself," Dad said. "I'm afraid something might happen to him. We have room. Maybe he could move in with us."

So just before Christmas, Grandpa came to live at our house.

At first it was fun having Grandpa live with us. I could see him anytime I wanted. We played checkers at night or watched television together. He'd sit with me while I did my homework.

But Grandpa was forgetting more and more.

Grandpa's doctor told Mom and Dad, "Grandpa has a brain disease that makes him forget. It's called Alzheimer's disease. Slowly, as time passes, Grandpa will forget more and more. He isn't going to get any better. But you can help him by gently reminding him of the things he must do. And by seeing that he is active, and safe, and does as much for himself as he can do."

When Mom explained this to me, I asked her, "Will you or Dad get this disease?"

She said, "Most people don't get it. But Alzheimer's disease happens to some older people. The doctors don't know why it happens. But they're trying hard to learn more about it."

"Was riding bikes with me bad for Grandpa?" I asked. I was afraid that somehow I had caused Grandpa's disease.

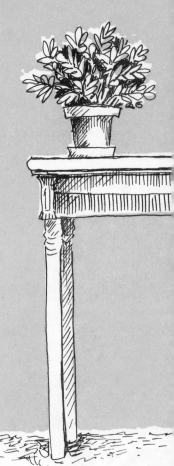

Mom held me tight and said softly, "It was nothing you did, Elizabeth. It's no one's fault. And now that we understand that Grandpa has Alzheimer's disease, we can take good care of him."

One winter day, when it was very cold, Grandpa went for a walk.

He forgot the way home.

My Dad and I found him just a few blocks from the house.

"I couldn't remember which way to go," Grandpa said. "I thought I was lost." He was looking all around him in a scared sort of way.

Dad took his arm and led him home, pointing at things along the way that Grandpa knew.

"See that house with the blue shutters, Grandpa? That belongs to the Johnsons ," Dad said. "And this is Maudie Simpson's house. Maude Simpson used to work with you at the post office."

After that day, Grandpa didn't go for walks
anymore. He walked around and around the house
instead. Some nights Grandpa couldn't sleep. He
was up late moving around. We locked all the doors
so he wouldn't wander away.

It seemed funny how instead of Grandpa taking
care of me, I was taking care of Grandpa.

As time went by Grandpa became more mixed up
and confused. One day in summer he went out in
his coat, two shirts, and shoes that didn't match.

He forgot where he was, and who we were.

"I want to go home! Take me home right now,"
he would say.

Grandpa didn't know us, so I'd remind him
slowly and gently.

"I'm Elizabeth, your granddaughter, and you *are*
home. You're living with us now, Grandpa."

Sometimes Grandpa hid things because he thought we would take them. Then he couldn't remember where he put them.

Once he got angry with me. "You took my watch," he said. "I know you took it."

I went to the nightstand and opened the drawer. "Here's your watch, Grandpa." It was in the same place it always was.

I began to cry. I couldn't help it. Grandpa cried, too. We both felt sorry about this illness which made him forget.

Mom and Dad worked hard taking care of Grandpa. They helped him dress, gave him baths, and took him to the bathroom so he wouldn't forget. But Grandpa didn't get any better.

Our family needed some time off from taking care of Grandpa. Our town has a center where Grandpa goes on Tuesdays and Thursdays. The people who run it like Grandpa. They work with him and try to keep him busy and happy. Grandpa is with other people who have Alzheimer's disease.

At the center they take care of him for the day, and at night he comes home to our house.

DADDY   MOMMY   ME

On the other days we take care of Grandpa. I try
to help as much as I can. Grandpa doesn't know
me any more. But I paint pictures for his room. I bring
him flowers from the garden.

And sometimes I just sit with Grandpa and hold
his hand so that he's not alone. He doesn't remember
who I am.

But I remember. I remember his house, the swing he made for me, our bicycle rides together, and the stories he told me.

I remember and I still love him.